The Licorice Daughter:

My Year with Ruffian

The Licorice Daughter:

My Year with Ruffian

Lyn Lifshin

Texas Review Press
Huntsville, Texas

FIRST EDITION, 2005

Requests for permission to reproduce material from this work should be
sent to:

Permissions
Texas Review Press
English Department
Sam Houston State University
Huntsville, TX 77341-2146

Acknowledgment:

So many people at different libraries and magazines were very
helpful, often sending me copies of out-of-print articles and sug-
gesting people to talk with, especially Phyllis Brown Rogers at
Keeneland Library, Diane Viert at Blood-Horse, Robert Weber at
National Sports Museum and Murray Bradley at Fairfax Library in
Vienna. Many sellers of Ruffian memorabilia, magazines and books
shared their thoughts and experiences seeing Ruffian, especially
Leo Collins, who sent me many fascinating articles and facts, and
Fred Arcara.

Cover painting of Ruffian by John Bellucci

Photograph of Lyn Lifshin by Jordan

Cover design by Paul Ruffin

Library of Congress Cataloging-in-Publication Data

Lifshin, Lyn.
  Licorice daughter : my year with Ruffian / Lyn Lifshin.-- 1st ed.
    p. cm.
  ISBN 1-881515-79-6 (alk. paper)
  1. Ruffian (Race horse)--Poetry. 2. Race horses--Poetry. 3.
Horses--Poetry. I. Title.
  PS3562.I4537L53 2005
  811'.54--dc22
                                  2005013637

The Licorice Daughter:

My Year with Ruffian

Ruffian . . . Her speed outpaced the cougar.
Her grace rivaled the Gazelle. In the long
history of horse racing, she was to be
only a moment's magic. But she had "the
look of eagles," which no one could forget.

—Dorothy Callahan

Ruffian

On April 17, 1972, at ten minutes to ten in the late evening, three days late, the only time she would be, Ruffian was born at Claiborne Farm in Paris, Kentucky. She was born with a star on her forehead, a sign of what she would become: the fastest filly, maybe the greatest horse of all time. From her record breaking maiden race, she left behind the best fillies and mares in races she ran and won almost effortlessly as she won stakes and broke records. She was ahead at every point of call. Ruffian was strikingly beautiful, more like his Black Stallion, the writer Walter Farley said, than any colt he'd seen, the image of The Black Beauty. An undefeated winner of lightning fast speed, Ruffian was Champion Juvenile filly of 1974. She was never headed, flew to breathtaking, stunning victories with a stride like no other horse, almost ghostly. Invincible until just after her Triple Crown win for fillies, it seemed Ruffian didn't know how to lose. Then, in a tragic, misguided match race with the winner of the year's Kentucky Derby, the colt Foolish Pleasure, she broke down, even then in the lead by nearly a length. Even on three legs, thrusting her broken foreleg into the ground over and over, she could not easily be pulled up.

No one who saw her can forget her. Ruffian was rare, perfect, spectacular, miraculous, bright, and she is buried where no other horse has been buried, where she ran her first and last race at the infield at Belmont under the NYRA flagpole, her nose pointing, as it always did, toward the finish line.

CONTENTS

Black Horses in Dreams
(Before Ruffian)

Small and New in the Lamp of Her Mother's Eye
(Ruffian's Birth)

Taken, Picked Like Unripe Fruit
(Weaning Ruffian)

As with Dancers the More Confident Fillies Were in Front
(Ruffian as a Yearling)

She Was Good To Be Around
(Ruffian as a Two-Year-Old)

Other Horses Turned to Jelly When She Looked Them in the Eye
(Ruffian as a Three-Year-Old)

Darkness Croons to Her Daughter
(Ruffian's Death)

Like Nothing We'll See Again
(After Ruffian)

Black Horses in Dreams
(Before Ruffian)

When I Think of the Horses Kept in the Dark of Mines

moving slowly through
candlelight, no green,
no sky or moon, and
how, coming into the
brightness above earth's
grave, they went crazy,
wild. It was too much
to take in, the quivering
leaves, scent of clover
and yarrow. The blaze
of sun frightened them
like horses who run
back to burning
buildings, terrified. In
their panic, they pick
the known, even if it
means death, like Ruffian
who only knew how to
fly to victory. Reined in,
in agony, the horses
battle what, like Ruffian,
trying to outrun what
scared her, blinds them

Horses in the Snow

if you are still, you
can hear ice crystals
move like beads
in blackness, before
you see them stand.
Under a snow maple
their legs lift in the
ballet step *pas de
cheval*, shake the
cold off, huddling
like children or the
memory of children,
shapes dark as
the space snow angels
leave, their hooves
an angel's tiara.
Light glosses the
grey as steam from
the horses rises

The Blue Horse Puzzle

the first horse in my
life long before my
sister and I collected
statues, went nightly
to the Morgan Horse
Farm to watch the foals.
This first horse, a white
stallion against a blue
sky he could fly through
like those Socony
horses, red as lips
and as seductive,
slicing air, towering
above cars and dogs,
prancing, tail wild
and proud. He was the
first animal I held,
kept pristine as none
of my child's books
were. There are no
stuffed animals, no
Barbies, no crossword
puzzles. Only this
proud wild horse,
tenderly kept and now
still in my own house
years later as if
I knew even then such
strength and beauty
would be rare

Morgan Horse Farm

June nights, our apartment
still warm even with the
breeze from Otter Creek,
we'd pile in the black
Plymouth, drive to the
horse farm. My sister,
horse crazy, her suit-
case packed to run
off to clean stalls at
Saratoga race track,
always ran ahead. I
wanted to see the
spindly colts and
fillies, how they
moved farther from
their mothers in the
field as I was afraid I
never would. Light
fell behind the
maples. For once,
since it was free, my
father wasn't scowling.
My mother beamed,
having us in the
bracelet of the
car, as close as those
horses nuzzling
each other, content
to let their small
world be the world

Sleeping with Horses

though I never have, I dream
of such warm flanks,
pulse of blood deep
enough to blur night
terror. I want my own
mare, sleek, night
colored to block
memories of the
orchard of bones,
the loved-lost under
leaves, under a quilt
of guilt. I think of
cats, long slept with
then gone, how
the Egyptians buried
not only wives but
their favorite pets
near them to cushion
their trip to the
underworld. I want
this mare, velvety
as the dream mare's
nose, nuzzling my
skin in the black
that braids us into
one so I won't
move unless she does

The Horse I Never Had

is the one I held
slithering onto the
new straw, watched her mare
quiver to, tongue.

This horse is like
no other, ballerina
with taut legs her mother
and I marvel at, holding
her own so soon,

hardly staggering.
The horse I do not
have will never, I'm sure,
lose her ebony sheen,
go grey or die

in the moon but will
graze in dreams, stand,
a dark statue in
snow fields, her tail

a swath of rhinestones,
watching for me to
slip her sugar, taste

her own taste
on my skin

The Horse Lullabies, the Insomnia

glistens in the
moon, dew still on
the wild vines. Her
mane brushes my
skin, a quiver of
danger through
curtain gauze,
the promise of
warmth, of
flight. It brushes
through blackness, a
sleekness behind
black pines,
the promise of
night flowers,
birds you don't
see in the light.
Hang on darling
the moon dares,
the arch of my
thigh, velvet as
shadows we'll
fly through.

The Young Girl Dreams of Escape

of a wild mane her
own hair tangles
with, her thighs
opening for the
horse's warmth.
She will elope
when the rest of
the house is sleeping,
carrots and apples
for her love.
She has cantered
through dreams of this,
the horse lover,
almost a part
of the harp of her
body. Night wind,
the mane a pillow
stars tongue.
This is not love
pressed up against
high school
lockers, a one
night stand in the
back seat but
a world suspended

Small and New
in the Lamp of Her Mother's Eye
(Ruffian's Birth)

With Blue Green Grass Holding Kentucky Night Water

at 9:50 April 17
she was there, suddenly,
dark and slick as she
would be on her
last night. Ruffian,
with a star on her
forehead, pale buds
outside the stall
door. She was lying
beside her mother
on the straw. Her
mare, Shenanigans,
still sweaty from
the birth though it took
less than half an
hour. The filly,
all long skinny legs,
awkward, bent, too
long it seemed for
the little body,
licorice but when
wiped down, a dark
chocolate with a
few grey hairs and
behind one left leg,
a white band, a
white bracelet
to go with the
star she'd be

Right After Birth

someone said she looked
big, more like a colt
than a filly. She wanted
to get to her feet right
away, kicked the straw
as she would again in
her darkest late night
later, always anxious
it seemed to be on her
way. She didn't seem
panicked or wild but
seemed to know she
could do it. Suddenly
she was on her feet,
awkward, stumbling
but she was standing
up and she was starved

First Day in the Light

eyes blinking in the
sun's glare. Tiny hoof
prints in soft earth.
Columbine, butter
grass. Each tiny leg
picked up as if to
test where she stood.
When her mother
trotted, the filly
trotted after her. When
Shenanigans nibbled
the sweet grass,
Ruffian stuck down
her nose and sniffed.
When her mother
turned to let the sun
warm her, Ruffian let
the light lick her
mane. For days, the
mare and filly slept
close to each other
in a paddock just for
them to keep the
baby safe as light
burned longer and the
two stayed longer
and longer in it

April 1972

after trees leaf out
and spiders spin a
lace of water and
rhinestones, the
horses move near
the fence, the foals
close to their mares.
Emerald light
haunts the trees,
the leafy gauze
soft as new grass.
Ruffian glues her
self to her mother
those first days
in the paddock,
won't let her
out of her sight

That First Summer

Ruffian ran free,
roamed meadow grass.
She nursed while
Shenanigans grazed.
As she grew bolder,
she explored the
paddock on her
own, nibbled at butter-
flies, played with
stablehands, ran back
to her mother if
something startled
her. Birds, leaves, a
wind of clover
and roses. Then the
coolness of a maple
or oak when the
summer day
grew sweltering

The Last Days in the Pasture, After the Hottest Days of Summer

when she rose up
on her delicate
hooves, pawing at
butterflies, a kicked
up ball of grass.
After days so slow
and full, lazying
in sweetness, the
Kentucky blue
grass shimmering,
a waterfall of light
and then the shade
to lie down and
rest in before fall,
when everything
would change.
Ruffian ran after
falling leaves.
She was big, she
was bigger than
most of the colts
and she was faster
than any of them

Just Before Weaning Day

all week, the horses
chased falling leaves

soon they would not
paw the air near
these roses,

everything was changing

goodbye to the blue chicory,
goodbye to their mares

the wind told them nothing,
the light seemed to be

shriveling, going

only the air had a smell of
frost and burning

burning to run, didn't yet
mean running from

all that still seemed
all there was

Taken, Picked like Unripe Fruit
(Weaning Ruffian)

Early, with Only Lanterns of Light

the dark gate creaks
open. Where there
were violets, the
first layer of rust
leaves. The horses
hear footsteps,
stiff weeds make
a noise like glass
shattering. The
horses are restless,
whinny, try to glue
themselves to
their mothers.
Wind of dead
roses and heart-
break. Wind of
the unknown, of
loss. The horses
go wild, pushed into
vans, not led to the
pasture, paddocks.
If Ruffian was a
wild filly she might
make her way
back to her old
stall. But when
the van she is
pushed into
clanks shut she
can't even
look back

Weaning Day—1

hinges creak on the gate.
Someone is coming too
early. Something is
unlatching the every
day, the warmth of her
mare, closeness of
her withers. Later, only
the road full of leaves
and stones. Something
is wrong. Their
mares can't save them.
Slats in the van. Colors
unseen in their six
months. Dust floats up
as if to blur everything
that was ordinary,
comforting. How could
the foals know, whinny-
ing and stamping, that
this happens every
year? Or that in the
new barn with only the
moon and stars for
company, in days they
would forget their mothers

With Starlight Still on the Pond Like Silver

the fillies' and mares'
heads curl back. A
whinny at one end
of the barn travels
to the other. The
horses want to hang
on to what is familiar.
But as stars go off
into cobalt sleep, the
men come to pull
Ruffian to the van on
her way to a new
life where she will

break records that
go back to the Civil
War to become a
horse that seems to
dance on water

Weaning Day—2

Today the barn
isn't a place
but the ghost
of a summer.
Today it dissolves
as if fire reached
through it turning
everything
familiar to ash.
The horses'
shrieks are flames
catching from
stall to stall.
The foals don't
want to leave
their mothers.
Terror blazes.
Mist over the
blue pond, a
smoke everything
ahead blurs in

Weaning Day—3

when the doors opened
they were in a new
place. Four other fillies
packed in the van, all
smaller than Ruffian.
Terrified and disoriented,
they had new clean hay
and food and water
but no mothers. The
new stalls too empty.
The fillies squealed.
Blue haze, a day of a
little death they will
survive before the others

In Their New Stalls

some nose out every
corner for their
mothers, rise up,
bleat, kick the
doors screaming.
Later, they will
lie down in new
straw, their first
night alone after
whinnying as loud
as they could,
ears back for the
answering cry

Now the Pastures Are Empty

the mares stand alone in their stalls.
Those who've lost their foals
for the first time paw the hay,
sniff for something familiar.
Moments before, the barn full of
shrieks and neighing, a dark
truck backfiring. Ruffian dug her
tiny feet into the hay, tried to
nuzzle her mare, her long legs black
as the bones of cherry branches.
She was born as the petals opened,
stood close to her mother in the
shade, is gone before light
comes

Ruffian's Last Weanling Month

air chill, especially for Kentucky.
The barn must have seemed

dark, the day of least light coming.
Even with early shadows, the

fresh cold must have made her
dance, scuffle frosted leftovers

in the garden. I think of her pawing
dried leaves, iced hairs of grass

as she darts after crows in
the snowflakes, free, her tongue

catching the crystals

Ruffian, If I Had Seen You at the Fence

would I have fed you
apples in December,

a weanling's last gift?
And would you have tilted

your head back, whinnied
as the shadows got colder

and the bits of pink
from your jaws

the only color

As with Dancers
the More Confident Fillies Were in Front
(Ruffian as a Yearling)

To Start, They

touch their ears so they
won't freak when
touched. Shenanigans'
filly, from a line of
the wildest, squealed
at everything new,
was a quick study
but needed a space
without a name,
a boundary between
herself and her
trainers, a border you
could almost see
as if to remind you
her sire's sire was as
close to a wild
horse as a stallion
could be and
still be handled

Like Ballet Warm-up at the Barre

the yearlings start slowly.
A little walk, a little
jog, then some cantering,
like plies, tendus in
ballet before any leaps,
even before *petit allegro*.
Nothing glamorous, no
prima ballerina in the
training track, no one
looking for the next
Secretariat or Pavlova.
The young horses'
and dancers' bones
still soft and tender,
no one tested them,
they used their hands
and legs but it was
the voice, whispers,
sometimes singing,
reassuring, soothing,
helping the skittish
horses and would-be
ballerinas most who
no matter how cared for
could never be truly safe

By the Time the Horses File Around the Paddock

for days, the fillies
head over to the track.
Each day, something
different like trying
dancers in brand-new
choreography: which
lead with confidence,
which are nervous,
shy from shadows.
As with dancers
the more confident
fillies were in front
so the others could
watch and follow.
It was like walking
through a new piece of
dance, responding to
instructions, behaving,
learning not to bolt
or slow down, to
lay a foundation for
when someone might
become a star

For Ruffian, a Squeal, a Few Bucks

that's healthy, the grooms
said. A filly, she was a
tomboy, didn't go for
taking a bath, a sponge
bath was one thing but
she balked at a full bath.
Bigger and stronger
than the other fillies she
could do more damage
when she acted up. If
there was a film of
Shenanigans' dark girl,
frame by frame, she'd be
shaking her head at
the water, annoyed as
a cat, kicking at the
rainbow spray between
her legs, finally, as if
she'd made her point,
agreeing to just
go with it

After Days of Figure Eights in the Stall

after the bit, the martingale,
stirrups, after a few bucks
in the small palm of the
stall, a new barn, new trees,
new shadows. Inside, the
grooms led the full tacked
yearlings out into the small
paddock and led them around
in a circle, like children
walking the halls of a new
school where nothing feels
the same. Some are curious,
some cautious, some wild.
No one rushes the yearlings.
Light highlights the rusts
and licorice, mahogany and
coppery gold. Riders
watch in the sun, look for
a calm, steady baby for
the leader. One rider thinks
of the almost black yearling,
must have whispered
something calming like "be
a good girl," or "like a lady,"
as he took the rein and
Ruffian took a few steps
sideways, then, as if the star
on her forehead was
what she was becoming,
settled in
for the start

Her Beautiful Thin Strong Legs

too beautiful, too thin

gave her perfect
conformation. I think of

Ruffian's jockey,
balancing as if his toes

were a seesaw.
Taste of the horse's neck.

I imagine the stablehands
brushing Ruffian, her

hair in a brush would be
an eBay relic now

Some Nights I Think of Her

lying quietly all night

as if she knew, for the moment,
her body was her friend

A star on her forehead,
a star inside her blood

Herons in the distance,
gulls. Her star,

color of the
floating lily

Sky Colorless

as so many days must have
been at Claiborne Farm

Ruffian, prancing in the
pewter January light

Camellias about to open,
she was tasting the cold air

each lick, a kiss,
exotic as the taste of

a burning moon,
as jolting as moving

from pastures of
roses and owls

to a world of jockeys and
trainers, betters and gates

once you've left
you can't look back at

Yearlings in the Pasture

no responsibility, just play
in the grass in a rose wind,
a butterfly wind. Before
harnesses, before shoes,

velvety bodies push and
shove, roll on their backs
squealing, chasing, becoming
the color of that rusty earth

She Was Good To Be Around
(Ruffian as a Two-Year-Old)

It Was Her Stride, Long, Almost Dream-Like, Floating

riders with a sense of
pace were fooled.
She was like a dancer
with ballon, hanging
in the air, suspended.
If you were on her,
you thought the
clockers were wrong.
Sometimes it seemed
she wasn't running,
never came back
winded. Those long
legs seemed too
long for a real horse.
Someone said it
was as if she hung
there and the ground
rushed under her

Before She Had Her Name

she was Sophie,
the big sofa,
soul sister
because she
was black. No
one seemed
to know her
name, dark
mystery,
midnight. No
one knew if
even the clockers
knew. Speed-
ball beauty,
the female, the
freak. But
one hot walker
said she would
still be a stakes
filly, name
or no name

When I Look at Ryder's Painting, *The Race Track*

Death on a Pale
Horse, I see it reversed,
circling back. Horses
and death, the riderless
horse at JFK's
funeral, stirrups
going backward. That
May, Ruffian's
maiden, the tattoo
inside her lips
still new. I imagine
her muscles rippling
on that two-
minute gallop
to the gate, the blue
air, her mane
smelling faintly of
soap and apples. Metal,
silk, the gasp, thunder,
then one black
arrow whizzing past

Ruffian's Maiden Race

in her 12 by 12 foot stall
24 hours a day, Ruffian
nibbled playfully at
stable hands. A little
edgy. A little ready.
A race for horses who've
never won, her new jockey
took her out early,
could barely tighten the
reins. When asked, What
do you think?" jockey
Jacinto Vasquez said I
never rode a horse like
this. She knows what she's
doing. She wants to run
and I want to ride her

Just Before Ruffian's Maiden Race

the branches of apple trees,
snow petals falling on cars.
Ruffian's trainer put on her
bridle, must have felt his
heart race. He must have
held his breath, wondered
how Ruffian would do with
so many people, leaned
against her as shadows of
sea gulls darkened the grass.
Ruffian was calm some-
body says. You do good out
there her groom said,
just move along like he
tells you. Her head down,
walking her own walk,
cool, almost lazy, saving
her burning for the track

Ruffian, Her First Race

she stood calmly, her
only side step was when
the groom tightened
her girth. Then she
relaxed again. At
Riders Up, ten
horses spread out
around the paddock,
near each a bracelet
of people shaking
hands, grinning.
Ruffian warmed up,
relaxed, filed into
the gate from the
rail out. The jockey,
buried in her neck,
eyes ahead, knees
pressing her shoulder.
The gun and the
gates explode open.
Ruffian, one big jump
behind the first four
mounts out in front
cuts across the field
moves toward the rail.
Three lengths on the
closest horse. People
start jumping and
screaming. The horse
behind her tore from
the pack but she
was so far ahead
she glided over the
track, she was flying,
she was water over-
flowing what held it

That First Race in Black and White

few knew her name,
that May 22nd maiden.
Something in her
sparking like hot
wires. She was
winged, always
would be. Horse
angel, freak, so
far ahead of the
other fillies, camera-
men couldn't keep
both her and
the second horse
in the lens

She Was Transformed

after the gate opened,
after she broke a
little slow she exploded.
In that first race,
Ruffian finished fifteen
lengths ahead of all the
others. Her jockey
never touched his whip,
didn't touch her, just
let her run. Her speed,
supernatural, her
mane an ebony streak.
Papers said the greatest
race run by a first-
time starter

Sometimes It Seemed She Wasn't Real

a mystery horse
on invisible currents.
Even with a bad
start out of the
gate, even with the
jockey holding her
back she'd glide,
wild to overtake the
horses in front of
her. Even with
no shoes on to grab
the dirt she was
taking over, it was
as if she was some-
thing in a dream
in the shape
of a horse

Horse Tattoo

under the upper lip,
checked at each race.
Even Ruffian's tattoo
was inspected as if
you couldn't have
told as she broke
from the gates, her
almost black mane
glistening. Ever
controlled, her speed
was astonishing.
Still, she was only
playing. As soon as
her jockey asked for
a little more, she
drew away, red and
white stripes flashing

One Blacksmith Said He Could Pick up an Anvil with One Hand

but when he
would go in
Ruffian's stall
she didn't want
her tootsies
tampered with.
She'd back him
up in a corner
and make him
beg for mercy.
She had he said
a personality
to go along
with her size

You Can't Think Ahead

her trainer said,
can't get high on a
horse. After her
maiden, on through
summer as willows
yellowed and grass-
hoppers slivered
through silver reeds,
Ruffian won one
race after another,
breaking records.
The pink sun fell
into black water.
Super filly they
were calling her.
People talked about
her future. Shouldn't
count on too much
her trainer knew though
he was dreaming,
terrified sometimes
she was so fast

Saratoga, Ruffian's Cradle

but not her grave.
She danced to the gate
quivering with eagerness,
huge and glistening
as if she'd do this as
an old mare too.
The look of eagles
already in her eyes,
something past the
playful way she
nibbled maple leaves
on the way back to
the paddock. And too,
the hint she'd run her-
self to death, stagger to
the finish line on
three legs

Other Horses Turned to Jelly When She Look Them in the Eye (Ruffian as a Three-Year-Old)

Recovery, After Ruffian's Hairline Fracture

scratched, down for the
rest of 1974, Ruffian
recovered in her stall.
Sometimes she pushed
her feed tub, annoyed
she had less food since
she wasn't running.
She surprised every-
one, accepted confine-
ment in her stall. By
November, night
frost turned stones to
rhinestones, the breath
of horses and riders
making fog against
the green black pines.
Finally by December,
Ruffian was let out of
her stall. On the second
day, she walked for
an hour and a half
in the afternoon.
Brought to a small
paddock so she could
be free she started
to run, she was so
excited, kicked up her
back legs, reared and
pawed the air. By
the 3rd time she put
a fore leg over the edge
of the big fence
her trainer knew this
couldn't work, that she'd
have to be hot walked
even there

In Camden, Ruffian Tossing

her mane, wild to feel
it flow faster, a wake
in sea, invisible sails
lifting her. She wants to
be airborne, dark
and dreaming, wants
to burn. If she knew she
was injured, she has
forgotten. The crows can
take off, leap where
they want, sun on their
wings, on her wings. She
is aching to get going.
Even in the small paddock,
Ruffian starts from a
standstill, leaps forward,
tears around the paddock
heading toward the fence,
wild to play, to run
after months of healing.
She leaps around, inches
from a head on crash
and disaster as her
groom holds his breath
and like a ballet dancer
turning so fast she blurs
across the stage, she
stops right on balance

By March Ruffian

was running strong.
She was fierce,
bright as the red
tulip of the inside
of her mouth. She
was still the beauty,
the heartbreaker.
She was energy
in black lightning.
She was rested,
ready. The moon
lit up the star on
her forehead. She
was ready to be
star, fire, beauty.
In her first race
back, she led
the closest horse
by five lengths. The
queen was going to
the New York
Triple Crown

Ruffian

huge lungs and heart,
all the better
to never sweat with

a wide forehead
for beauty

walking on what
for humans would
be their toes,

walking like a
ballerina,

no foot
no horse

Everything about Ruffian
beautiful, big

but her feet
a little small

and her cannon bone,
a beautiful bracelet

unwilling to give

Spring of Ponds Near

the track with the dragon
flies hovering, spring
of her black beauty,
her fire, her ghostly
speed. Later some
will say she struck
herself down, what
made her great
destroyed her. Spring,
too short with light
starting to leave.
Spring of humming-
birds, or cherry dust
like the first snow.
Spring Ruffian breezes
from the gates, leaps
over every finish line.
Then the musky
nights of cats in the
stall, mice and blue
birds, the late frosts
etching what was
too young to die

I Never Like To Stay Too Far Away from Ruffian—1

Jacinto Vasquez

If Ruffian could
learn to relax, if she
could be like a woman
with her lover. If she
trusted his touch,
could read the pull
of the bit like the
braille of his body,
each time a little more,
each stroke a whispered
story. If he could not
see her except as part
of his body, a ship to
gather in the sail
unfurling behind them
in a storm they could
only get through together

I Never Like To Stay Too Far Away from Ruffian—2

Jacinto Vasquez

As if, after he'd teased
her, after they teased and
taunted each other, jockey
and horse were moving
into the same flame,
the wind a kiss and his
body on her, a seduction.
They were molding,
they were melding. He
couldn't keep her from
taking him so fast she
couldn't keep his touch
from becoming more
fire-like, ecstatic as they
flew on their way to myth

After Angel Cordero Tried To Tire Out Ruffian, Exhaust Her Early

After Jacinto kept her from running out of steam before the wire,
after the bit tore her mouth
she was wild to keep coming

After her jockey controlled her, wouldn't let
her open the lead she wanted,
the bit tearing her mouth

After they approached the stretch, two lengths in the lead.
After Ruffian was easing away.
After she was so far in front, showing no fatigue.

After they crossed the line Jacinto didn't rise in the stirrups the way
the crowd expected but kept going on an extra eight though there
was no need
as if he and the horse had to have their say

Cordero's horse was tired, drifting into the weeds.
After Jacinto kept her from running out of steam before the wire.
After the winner's circle, the jockeys insulting each other in Spanish,
cursing the other's deeds

Ruffian was cool, still wild to keep running

I Never Like To Stay Too Far Away from Ruffian—3

Jacinto Vasquez

he couldn't not
be pulled toward
her as if something
unsaid lured him
to dance across
black pines, be
her father, her
lover. Did he
worry, wonder
why in so many
photographs
Ruffian leads
with that right
foot, as if to
reach what was
beyond the
finish line

Ruffian in the Winner's Circle

her shoulders glistened
like onyx, her fine cut
veins stood out along
her neck but if you
wanted to see her
sweat, you'd have to
throw her in the hot
box with her jockey

What's Next

after she won and won
with machine like precision,
with beauty and style, papers
asked what's next. Everyone
had an idea. Some thought
of races normally absurd
for a three year old filly.
Someone said she'd enter
the Belmont. Some thought
she'd take on colts soon.
Some thought a colt who
won the Derby and the
Preakness would be
wild. Some whispered
"match race." Some
thought in Alabama, The
Travers, the rich Marlboro
cup. Ruffian was the
glamor horse still and
everything was possible

When There Was Nothing Left for Her To Prove

when before her last dark
lurked, even as apples
ripened and roses
still perfumed thick
New York air. Before
anything sinister, before
black water filtered
down to sugar bones.
When the berries were
still glistening and
the lake, a night mirror,
she was heading to
her last victory, gleaming
and dark and huge,
dancing toward the
American Oaks, walking
the walk only she
could

In the Blue Pewter Air

Light rain. Inside the
barn, dark shapes
of horses, ghost
shapes in the blue
pewter air. In the rain,
perfume of clover
and hay. Hot walkers
cool horses, Ruffian's
groom cleans her
stall. Click of metal
shoes. Manure
and roses. Ruffian
thrusts her head
forward as if to
harness the day
as her groom goes
over her black
coat with a rub
rag, polishes her
to onyx. Ruffian
twists and flicks,
shifts her weight
in grey dampness
where later her
hoofprints
fill with rain

She Wanted To Run, a Fast Dance

she seemed to be getting
faster with each race,
went straight to the
front. No one could
hold her back, the black
glow, a ghost sailing
faster than you supposed.
Hovering in the air
as if part of the air, not
earth, not from the
earth. Only what
made her win could
bring her back to it

That Last Spring Ruffian Was Ghostly

freakish speed no
filly passed for
more than seconds.
By June, there were
no more fillies to
beat. Sparrows
sang in her stall,
roses were dripping.
She was winged,
she was supernatural.
Crowds wanted a
match race. No one
cared about betting,
just what horse
was the best, the
gorgeous filly,
the Derby colt. For
a match race, it's
stamina and will.
As swallows dipped
over fields, publicity
ballooned. A race
between a boy and a
girl, the race of the
century, with Ruffian
the favorite

She Was the Wonder, the Big Filly

no other horse
has a claim of
the big soul
black filly,
no one has
beaten her
dancing in the
wind, swooping
like plush
licorice velvet.
The queen
of every race,
too perfect
for death to not
want to
dance with

An Onyx Bundle of Energy

You couldn't believe how strong,
        how huge Ruffian was
until you stood right up close.
Look at those hind quarters her
        trainer said,
that's where she gets that throughst

Right up close, she was enormous
        and fast but she had such an
        easy way of going.
Sometimes a yearling looks great
        but the others catch up.
But not with Ruffian. She was perfectly
        made for speed and thrust. It
        always looked easy.
From the beginning, she was special

Those other yearlings never caught
        up with her.
Copernica never ran the same after
        Ruffian beat her.
From the start her trainer knew.
A big filly, but fine boned, perfect proportions

Like Copernica, so many fillies were never
        the same when they lost to Ruffian.
In a decade, the 70s, full of stars,
she was special. Perfect. A perfect lady.
Girls can be ruffians too her owner said

With so many famous 70s horses, Secretariat, Affirmed,
        Ruffian is still the heartbreaker.
Secretariat's trainer said as God is my judge,
        Ruffian might be better.

"She was a nicest filly, but a handful," her trainer
    said, "she was a joy but she was a ruffian."
Other horses turned to jelly when she looked
    them in the eye

It Always Ends the Same Way

But in the days before the
Match Race everything was
still ahead, wildly exciting.
July 6, the sky was pewter.
Everyone hoped the rain
would hold off. Ruffian
never ran on mud before.
No one knew how she'd
do if it got soaked and
sloppy. Leaves curled
inward in the wet dark
wind. Air threatening,
heavy. The horses were
checked, pulse, heart-
beat and temperature,
normal. No sign of
lameness. The audience
was relieved, settled
back, knew the odds
favored "the girl," that
even if she won, they'd
never turn in those tickets
but would keep them
for souvenirs of the
great race of their lives

On the Day of Ruffian's Match Race

it began to sprinkle
after the 4th race.
Everyone gasped,
held their breath.
4 o'clock in the
afternoon, the jockey
was getting dressed.
Charcoal sky at
4 o'clock. Only
two jockeys, only
one could win. The
air still heavy as
other horses thundered
past. 4 o'clock
moving toward 5. In
stable 34, the day
began like any
other. Ruffian's
food tub was
cleaned out. She
wanted to play. It
was grey, it was pewter.
Ruffian lifted a foot
and bowed her head.
She was perfect,
the doctors said so.
She knew it herself.
Just look one stable-
hand said at the
way she stood there

Darkness Croons to Her Daughter
(Ruffian's Death)

On the Day of Her Last Race

it was so dark
and gloomy, many
thought rain would
cancel the race.
She rested in her
air conditioned stall,
her trainer with her,
stroking the filly's
neck, talking softly to
her. Her groom brushed
her hair till it was like
silk and satin. By the
time of the race, the
skies lightened, the
jockeys mounted,
the fans shouted.
In one photograph
of the big filly, her
legs look so dainty,
the horses a blur from
the gate. It was suddenly
quiet. Ruffian was on
the inside. Dirt flew,
her hooves pounding,
tearing up the track.
Neck and neck, then
Ruffian ran ahead
with no other horse
beside her, a glaze of
black light opening
a lead of several feet,
a sizzling speed. Her
jockey eased up,
afraid she'd burn out

near the half mile
mark. Ruffian was still
in the lead then she
stumbled, staggered,
almost fell. Her jockey
heard a sharp crack,
like when you break a stick

On That Day

it was as if she had
wings and then
the wings turned to
wax, were melting.
There was a hush,
seconds after the
wild cheers as
Ruffian edged
ahead. It was hot
and the roses were
dripping. The sun
kept on, as it did
with Icarus falling
from the sky on
melting wings. The
birds didn't stop.
When her jockey
pulled her up that
last night, everyone
who knew must
have covered
their eyes

July 6, 1975, That Day, Only Ruffian

didn't seem uneasy. Thunder,
the sky threatening. Something
in too many people's guts, some
thing bad her trainer said
later. 6 p.m. seemed so late in
coming. Then, the scream of
the crowd. She flicked her ears
back, following the sounds.
Then the two horses were burning, tearing up the track. Ruffian
stuck her nose out front, she
was aching to run, she was draw-
ing away. The crowd was screaming. Then the jockeys heard
something else, that crack like a
tree limb breaking, like an ice
shove tearing through wood. Foolish
Pleasure suddenly passed her.
"Ruffian has broken down,"
on the microphone. Stunned, the
nightmare real, unfolding. But
Ruffian wouldn't stop. Jacinto
tried to pull the filly up as fast
as possible. She refused, she
wanted to run, she had to run.
Pain was a blur she couldn't seem
to understand. She was pulling
away from the colt, she was
running on three legs. She was
burning, determined. Tears stung
Jacinto's eyes. She was so strong,
so wild to run. Jacinto begged her,
he was crying. She wouldn't
stop. She ignored him, ignored the

pain. The skin of her fetlock
ripped, the bones bursting through,
the wound was opening, tearing her
up, tearing her ankle, her ligaments
then her hoof dangled, useless

When the Ambulance Came

the vet shook his head.
She had run her ankle
into the ground, ran
on bloody ankles,
only splintered bone.
Blood gushed from
the wound. Ruffian
reared in pain. Every-
one who could, tried to
hold her gently as they
could. Then the limping,
trembling filly, gorgeous
and proud moments
before, was led into the
ambulance, rivers of
sweat running down
her body, her eyes,
wild, a trapped
animal

After She Pulled Up, After the Blood Was Drying on July

after the crowd
went silent, after
it seemed hours
for the other
horse to move
over the track,
unbroken as
she was broken.
After the whole
country's
daughter collapsed,
a black heap of
pain, dark
grave of
disbelief,
burial of beauty

After the Accident

her groom and rider
stayed with her,
sneaking in past the
guards. They had to
be with her, knew
Ruffian as well as
anyone, knew she'd
be hard in her terror
and pain, knew if
anyone could ease
her maybe they could.
It was the sixty-year-
old trainer, if anyone
could, who could
calm her. And be-
cause Ruffian needed
him, he raced as
he never had to her

She Was Jumping Around

rearing in terror. The
track vet tried to put a
cast on her, gave her lots
of rein. He kept talking
to her, trying to calm
her. He was covered with
blood. The man who
loaded her into the gate
for most of her starts
felt sick to his stomach.
He knew how proud
she was, how bright and
smart and fearless and
he saw the look in her
eyes, that she knew how
bad it was, that he
could do nothing

Her Jockey Moved in a Blur

hardly knew what
he was doing, reached
under the filly. He
wasn't aware, there were
things he did so many
times, unbuckling
a girth, sliding off a
saddle. Up close he saw
her sweat soaked hair. She
had never broken a
sweat. He could smell
fear from her body.
All night when he couldn't
sleep, he'd felt things
wouldn't go well,
never dreamed this

After the Ambulance Ride Ruffian Bled So Inside the Cast the Cast Broke from the Pressure

of the blood. The vet
put on a second cast, at the
barn. Ruffian could not
walk by herself, had to be
urged, had to be half carried.
Chaos bloomed in the
stable. Ruffian was going
through cycles of terror, shock
and pain. They had to cool
her, gave her shots, half
carried her to the stall
where the vet x-rayed her,
rushed to the clinic to have
film developed. Every step
seemed endless. Her trainer
got the stable hands to
bring ice water, tub after
tub, bathing Ruffian's leg
while they held her up.
The drugs and ice were
cooling her off. She wanted
to lie down. The men
struggled to keep her up.
Once she was down,
she might never stand again

As Ruffian Slept

doctors repaired
muscles, tendons
and bones. Some-
one made a brace
so Ruffian could
stand up soon
after surgery,
something to hold
the weight of her
body. Someone
designed a
special shoe with
bolts in it. When
the surgery was
over, the support
bars would be
sealed in plaster.
The surgeon cut
into Ruffian's fore-
leg, removed bits
of shattered bone,
put drains under
the skin to carry
away the fluid,
picked out tiny
bone fragments
lodged in joints
and tendons. Her
groom and her
trainer knew even
if repaired, the
final choice was
up to her

When I Think of the Recovery Stall

the door set in the wall, how it
dropped so the top was flush
with the operating table. I
think of Ruffian on that ramp,
her great weight sliding into the
recovery stall, the air thick,
heavy with wet leaves. When I
think of the floor of straw
waiting to hold her, how she lay
there twenty minutes, I want to turn the
clock back. I want to have something supernatural as she was
to calm her. I don't want to
imagine how she struggled more
and more violently even though
the men tried to hold her down,
hitting the walls with her feet
as if she thought she was still
galloping

Maybe Because She Was Born Three Days Late

nothing in her would let her
not get to the finish line early.
No matter she was running,
pulling from anesthesia
as if the wind still
was unfurling behind her,
as if something like a sail
was lifting her ghostly
over the ground and the
crowd still asleep was
rooting for her. She was
still swooping, she was lying
on the hay. Nothing could
hold her. The finish line
gleaming. She wouldn't be
late again

After She Broke Through

the cast, after they
tried to save her,
not because they
really thought they
had a chance but
were buying time
for a miracle. After
almost everyone who
had been with her as
long as she was
alive, as long as they
could do something
for her could not
let her die. After
even her trainer
knew his limits. It
was twenty minutes
past two. Rain
had begun. Get
her halter for me,
he asked as they
stepped into the night.
One groom knelt
beside her, held the
filly's head while
the vet prepared a
shot of phenobarbital.
She was starting
to run again, she was
leading with her
right leg as she had
been in the race,
reaching with her
head, not fully
conscious as if
finally she could run

As if She Was a Piece of Sky

they tried to
hold. Her eyes
must have said
this, told them
she was wind
and you could
never hold wind
forever. Horses
run from pain
back to the
comfort of what
is familiar, back,
for Ruffian,
to the race, to
running. That
night she must
have seen what
no one could
imagine lying
down in her
thrashing as if
in some other
world she'd have
time to be still

After Midnight

death built her
long ship, pulled
her dark sails
over the filly
who ran as if
she had sails
at her back.
She was winged
and then she
was in death's
sails, leaving
a wake of black
lilies on her
way to the peace
that must have
come when
snow mounded
over what lives
in myth

Years Before Earth Beetles Have Made Lace of Her Lovely Bones

Stillness went into her
like reins pulling

her up at the finish line.
The anesthesia gone,
the thrashing. After her

gorgeous legs
stopped lashing and
striking out and her
heart no longer blazed,
her ebony muscles

froze and sweat was
wiped from her slackened
form. Ruffian, who never
sweated, who glided, effortless,

a black magic ship over earth,
her huge heart, her beautiful
head rolled to one side

Though She Didn't Run for the Roses

I think of the one rose dropped
into her stall size grave, of the
petals clotting over her grave as
they swamped Cleopatra's
bower. I think of the children
clutching roses later at Ruffian's
grave, of the flowers at Saratoga,
at Belmont. Everyone said how
she loved to run. Then I think of
someone saying babies shouldn't,
their bones still not formed or
strong, shouldn't be pressed to
run farther, faster. I think of the
beauty at the track, the sun on
jade grass. But when I think of
Ruffian's last hours, I don't think
roses but funeral flowers

Her Whole Body Was Buried

the grave twelve feet wide and twelve feet deep

people went to work
at the barn on Monday
morning. It was hard
but they did it. No
one believed what
had happened. The
hardest thing was
to take the horses
to the track. They
were digging Ruffian's
grave in the infield.
Walking by, you
just couldn't look.
One groom said all
the way to the 8th pole
you just could
not look

July 7, 1975—1

no horse will ever
stand in this stall again

her trainer Whiteley said.
No horse will be worthy

When the last racing fan
left Belmont that night

a huge bulldozer
rolled in, reaching

Ruffian's grave. The last
rose and guava light

gone, the horse van stopped
at the stop just beyond

the finish line,
her last race over

She Was Buried Just as the Last Light

failed, a little after
9. Two hours
earlier, a shovel
pulled up near the
flagpole, spit out
huge shovels of dirt,
made a hole about
the size of the stall
Ruffian lived in
all her life, twelve-feet
square. Though reporters
were banned from the
gravesite, they sat
up in the club house.
The ambulance door
lowered to form a
ramp right into the
pit at the base of
the flagpole. Many
were stunned to
see Ruffian wrapped
like a huge mummy.
Some wanted to see
that star again, the
white band circling
her left hind leg.
Her elegy was silence

July 7, 1975—2

In stillness
Ruffian was slid
into her grave,
12 by 12, the
size of the stall
she always lived in

before the earth,
her trainer gave her
groom the filly's
two red blankets,
the good ones
embroidered with the
initials of Locust Hill Farm
in bright white letters
in the corner

knelt beside the
white wrapped form
the lifeless body of the
filly he loved
wanted it perfect
since she was

then someone took a single
long stemmed rose
lifted from a box of flowers
stepped to the edge of the grave
and dropped it

it landed without a sound
by Ruffian's head

Rain, the Cherry Petals Going Pale Rose Snow

When I think of Ruffian's
trainer holding a pair of
red and white blankets
in stillness at her open grave,
I think of July night
scent rising up from the
lake and hedges in the
infield lawn at Belmont.
It was almost nightfall.
There was nothing left
to do but cover her remains
with the blankets, begin
living with the memories.
When I imagine 9:15 light,
darkness moving in, how
clouds parted overhead,
the sky tinged blue as on
the night Shenanigans
gave birth to her. I think of
the distant light of the club
house and grandstand
flickering on those at the
grave: Ruffian's jockey,
Jacinto Vasquez, in a suit
and tie, Ruffian's groom.
I think of Ruffian's
trainer, pale and his wife
holding a bouquet of roses,
the blankets draped over his
arm. When I think how
they couldn't save her
from herself, I think of
him, chalk faced with
her on the ambulance, in
the barn, the hospital and
now here, just standing
holding her blankets

Like Nothing We'll See Again
(After Ruffian)

Her Jockey's Song

She's like a gold-plated Cadillac.
Like a Caddy, when you ask her
     for more gas.
One trainer said as God was his
     judge she might be better
     than Secretariat.
She would make any jockey look good.

Like a Caddy, she was right there
     when you asked for more gas.
She had more gears than almost
     any horse.
You didn't have to do anything. She
     made any jockey look good.
When I ride her, I feel I can do anything.

She had more gears than any horse.
In a decade of top-heavy stars, she was
     the Queen.
When I rode her, I could do anything.
Sometimes a yearling looks great but the
     others catch up, but not
     with Ruffian.

In a decade full of stars, she was the Queen.
From the beginning they said she
     would be special.
Sometimes a yearling looks great but others
     catch up.
The lengths behind her unfurled like a carpet.

From the beginning, they said she would
     be special.
She seemed to float, suspended in air.

The lengths behind her flowed out like a carpet.
When she broke down, all over America
    little girls sobbed in their beds.

She seemed to float, as if she had wings
    or sails.
When Ruffian left the gate with Foolish
    Pleasure they matched stride for stride
    as if there was only one horse running

The shattered ends of the splintered bone
    cut through the skin.
To walk by her grave was harder
than seeing one set of footprints in the fresh
    track where there should have been two

Shattered, the Licorice Daughter

When Charismatic broke down someone said
        we don't want another Ruffian deal.
After Ruffian's death, all over America
        little girls were sobbing.
Speed could do that to a horse,
the good always get hurt, sooner or later

After Ruffian's death, nuns who had prayed,
        little girls, all were crying.
The bad racers never run hard enough to
        do their bodies wild harm.
The good ones live to run, get hurt, what
        makes them win, kills them.
So much pounding, so many shattered sesamoids.

The bad horses don't live to run, don't run
        hard enough, wouldn't run on the
        stumps of bloody ankles.
When Ruffian broke down, she transcended
        the world of racing.
Her sesamoids shattered, each time her
        ankle hit the track dirt and sand were
        shoved into the open wound.
What made her great destroyed her.

When she broke down, she became
        larger than life.
Her perfect record, the licorice daughter,
        beauty, filly freak, queen.
What made her great killed her.
On Ruffian's last day, like today, sparrows
were flying through the eaves at Belmont

When I Think of the Jewish Mourning Custom

I think of the guardians
watching over a dead
body, giving the soul
comfort and company
before the burial. I
think of the children
singing hymns for
Ruffian, nuns who
rarely come to the
track keeping all
night vigil. Some
wouldn't know she
was dead until the
light. They were like
those guardians. Some
one was washing
her, wrapping her
in white linen like a
shroud, modest as at
a Jewish burial. If
anyone has a soul,
Ruffian's must have
been eased, the pain
and terror gone as
roses browned in
New York heat where
her trainer, everyone
who loved her would
have used their
own bodies to protect
her from getting
to this

Ruffian, Whole and Gorgeous in Photographs

a beauty 13 lengths ahead of
all the fillies. How she never
trailed. How she . . . . Don't think
now of that hideous July,
muggy thunder in the air,
think how even in her first
race, May 22, over thirty
years from this melting day,
she opened up three lengths,
was in front down the stretch,
wild to the wire, a fifteen-length
winner. She was cool as a
jazz horn player, hardly
broke a sweat. People shook
their heads as if listening
to Miles Davis. Think instead
how she equaled the track
record in her very first start,
how that wasn't a fluke.
Think of her beauty, massive,
a giant, a gorgeous big girl.
Do a riff for her perfection,
feminine style, for how she
walked, how she could
have been such a brood mare.
Moan for Shenanigans. And
Ruffian's sire, Reviewer,
with his injuries and speed,
never out of the money.
Blues for the match night,
that black tunnel. Blues for
Ruffian racing from the past
and from her future

Watching *That Horse*, as Her Trainer Always Called Her, on Tape

I can see why they called
her "Wonder Lady."
People who saw her
said her walk was
unique. No one didn't
call her special. I
keep going back to
the opening shot of
Belmont, hazy,
mysterious early
light where Ruffian
started and ended.
Years later, her trainer's
face is still full of love
and if he was a
crying man, talking
of her first and
last day, he'd be sobbing

Another Horse Would Have Become Dog Food

become grass, been
gulped by cows, turned
rib eye. For Ruffian,
time is a knife slicing
a maple, letting
sweetness flow.
What seemed color-
less turns redolent as
her dark bay mahogany
eyes. Her muscles
float over the Internet
on eBay, don't lose
their shimmer,
the power some
would give more than
you can imagine
to have back

With the Craze To Keep Something of Ruffian, Even Her Brother Icecapade's Photo

on eBay goes
for $300.
"A treasure," the
write up says,
the world's lead
sire, best known
as the older
brother of
Ruffian. I think
Pere Lachaise
cemetery in
Paris, flowers and
gin around Jim
Morrison's grave,
lovers posing
even in the rain,
wonder if,
besides flowers on
Ruffian's grave
anyone brings her
favorite oats

Early Morning at the Track,
the Grass Rhinestoned, Luminous

those watching could
have watched her forever,
her power and beauty
rubbing off on them.
Sometimes it seems
they'd seen too much
to want to watch
another horse, get
used to what has flashed
by not being still with
them or walk away from
all tracks the night
the myth of her
freakish speed be
came air, floating light
as moths over the horse
shoe wreath of carnations

She Ran Like a Fawn

running from flames
for its life, something
leaping into water.
For her the finish
line was the tree
Daphne threw her-
self into. Ruffian was
black fire. She was
blackness sailing over
water. She wore the
sky on her withers,
stars on her forehead.
She was her own
jewel. I was scared
her trainer said, every
time I sent her on
to the track. She
couldn't stop using
herself up. The best
run hardest no
matter if it kills
them. Some still
dream under the horse
shoe wreath, the
dust of white
carnations, Ruffian
gallops through the dark

She Was a Dancer

She was in the bloodline
of Native Dancer. She
was the kind of
dancer who couldn't
stop, would have danced
or run on a railroad
with engines coming at
her to be out in
front. She was a strong
dancer but delicate,
was like a ballerina
whose tendon tears
under black tights so
no one sees the blood,
a dancer who keeps on,
a dancer who cares
more for the crown than
any pain, dancing,
running on blood, tear-
ing herself up for
those yelling her name

Now Ruffian Is Nibbling Apples from a Tree They Never Shrivel or Drop from

Now she is sniffing
new hay, the clean
blue air. In this
new life of
maple leaves,
no fences. She
nuzzles the
foal she never
had, a filly,
a dark beauty
like her, a
princess of fillies.
Together they
bend to clear
water then gallop,
leap and run
where there
is no track

In the Photographs on the Mantel

her dark mahogany coat.
Sometimes I look at her
sleek body, almost too
delicate legs as if I could
pick the lock to what she
was thinking in the shots
leaning into each other
as if to unchain something
nobody knows from the
blackness. I feel her
eyes when I sit down to
try to type, when I lie
in the quilt and can't
sleep. I rename my cat
Jete Pentimento Ruffian,
a girl but a ruffian too,
a beauty and fast. I
imagine Ruffian in her
earth bed, the moon in
grass over her, pale light
filtering to her bones,
the silent roses. If I think
of her restless in her
buried stall, striking
out for a gallop under
tree roots and the under-
sides of flowers I can
almost hear the last
sounds they would play
back, not the operation
room drone or the
pleading whispers that
she keep the cast where

they put it but the music
of those in the bleachers
yelping, "Go, Ruffian, go"